Piano · Vocal · Guitar

THE ORIGINAL CARTER FAMILY

CONTENTS

Cover photo courtesy of Country Music Hall of Fame
Interior photos courtesy of Country Music Foundation Library and Media Center,
Nashville, TN., Maybelle Carter, Ralph Peer, II.

www.peermusic.com

ISBN 0-634-00381-X

HAL•LEONARD®
CORPORATION
7777 W. BLUEMOUND RD. P.O. BOX 13819 MILWAUKEE, WI 53213

Visit Hal Leonard Online at
www.halleonard.com

1. Early publicity photograph

THE ORIGINAL CARTER FAMILY

The original Carter Family playing and singing group was made up of three people, A.P., Sara, and Maybelle. The style of the Carters was comprised of two parts which blended to make the total effect: first, the intricate use of the guitar as a lead instrument (which was an innovation at the time of their beginning), and second, the vocal harmonies.

Alvin Pleasant Delany "Doc" Carter, the oldest of eight children, was born to Robert and Molly Bays Carter on December 15, 1891. A.P.'s father was a banjo player, and he met his future wife, Molly, at a square dance. After their marriage, he gave up the instrument, as he gave up many of his worldly ways because of his religious views. Oft times mountain musicians, upon conversion, would begin playing religious music only, but in the case of A.P.'s father, he gave up the banjo altogether.

For her part, Molly Carter brought into the family many old ballads that had been handed down for years and years, songs like *SAILOR BOY, BROWN GIRL,* and *SINKING IN THE LONE-SOME SEA* which the Carter Family would later record.

A.P. Carter spent a year in Indiana working on a railroad gang near Richmond. A soldier of fortune and a jack of all trades, he often traveled far and wide seeking his fortune. He made his home wherever he found it, but his heart was really on Clinch Mountain, Virginia. He returned to his mountain home in 1911 and began selling fruit trees for a living, but during his years away from the hills of Virginia, A.P. had begun writing songs about his life as he knew it back at his Clinch Mountain home.

On one of his many trips around the area selling fruit trees, he met Sara Dougherty, born July 21, 1899. According to family legend, she was singing *ENGINE ONE-FORTY-THREE* and playing the autoharp at the time they met. Although A.P. and Sara had known one another earlier, the autoharp meeting flowered into the beginning of a courtship, and later into marriage on June 18, 1915. Almost from the beginning they made music around their household at Maces Springs, Virginia.

Sara had learned to play the autoharp from Eb Easterland and purchased her

2. Sara Carter
3. A.P. Carter
4. Maybelle Carter

5.

6.

7.

8.

instrument from one of the mail order companies; the autoharp was a very popular instrument of the day. A.P. played the fiddle, as he continued to do throughout his life, although every time his fiddling was mentioned to him he apologized for his lack of ability. During the early years of their marriage, A.P. and Sara sang and played in home groups and at places such as local schools and churches. To supplement his income as a nurseryman, A.P. farmed and did blacksmith work and carpentry.

A.P. and Sara Carter were a striking couple—both of them tall, strong, thoroughbred-looking mountain stock. A.P. Carter was said to have had a personal magnetism that was remarkable. "His presence filled the room," someone once said. He was a kind, gentle person, but full of fire when angered. Sara was a strikingly beautiful woman, a proud lady with head erect and shoulders straight, and with eyes that seemed to look right through you. Her voice was strong and pure, the beauty of the Appalachian dialect was never so enflowered as in the voice of Sara Carter.

The third member of the group was cousin Maybelle Addington, born on May 10, 1909. She was a little child when Sara and A.P. married, but with her

9. Maybelle's style of guitar playing was unique

ability on the autoharp, banjo, and guitar, she was the pride of the Addington clan and was quickly noticed by the Carters as she came onto the local music scene. As she grew up and assumed her role in the homemade

music world of Scott County, Virginia, her musical prowess was the talk of the county. "No one could pick it like Maybelle Addington," they would say, or "Honey, I hope you can learn to pick that thing like little Maybelle Addington can." In 1926 she married A.P.'s brother Ezra, and the Carter Family was complete. They played together a good deal in the past, but with the addition of Maybelle at Maces Springs, the availability of all members to practice was greater.

Maybelle purchased an L-5 Gibson guitar, an extremely expensive instrument in those days. It sold for $125.00. Her family was quite sure of her ability and had great faith that her talents would be recognized by others – therefore the substantial investment. Close examination of photographs of other musicians of the time doesn't reveal very many guitars of such quality. For the most part, they are nondescript mail order or bargain store instruments.

Maybelle's style of guitar playing was unique, and evidently she came up with it on her own. What she did was play the melody on the bass strings while maintaining a rhythm on the treble strings, fingering a partial chord. Later she developed some intricate melody runs on the bass strings. Of course, such

10.

11.

12.

runs were not new, but they were used differently by Maybelle, they were being used not only as part of the lead instrument, but as fills and also for the "bottom" of the song. Throughout it all, the strong emphasis on the bass was a must, and this was gained in part by the use of a thumb pick and two steel finger picks. Later, this style was to be imitated to the note by literally thousands of guitar players.

Maybelle played more than the guitar, though. She was fairly accomplished on the banjo and fiddle, as well as the autoharp, and a picking all-new styles. She played the autoharp in a way that it hadn't been played before. Rather than strumming across the harp while barring a chord, Maybelle actually picked out the melody with her thumb and finger picks.

The vocal part of the Carter Family sound was no less innovative. If you listen to the early hillbilly recordings, you find that, basically, the singers were barely singing over the instruments. The Carter style was built around the vocals and incorporated them into the instrumental background, usually made up of the basic three-chord structure. In essence, the Carter Family violated the main traditions of vocal and instrumental music, but in doing so created a whole new style and a whole new sound.

In July, 1927, an article on the front page of the *Bristol, Tennessee-Virginia News Bulletin* informed the public that a man named Ralph Peer was in town (Bristol) auditioning local talent. The paper was read daily by the Carters in Scott County. August 1, 1927 found the group together at the home of Ezra and Maybelle. Ezra Carter, a small, wiry, handsome, laughable, lovable young man, cut the last of last year's country ham and helped Maybelle prepare a big breakfast for A.P., Sara, and themselves. "Well, it looks like we're gonna have a bunch of radio stars around here," said Ezra.

"I don't know about that," said A.P. (Doc), "but it might be worth a trip to Bristol if we can get $50.00 to record a song like Ernest Stoneman did."

"Aw, pshaw," said Sara, "ain't nobody gonna pay that much money to hear us sing."

Young Maybelle kept silent; maybe she had her own dreams, her own ideas about how it was all going to work out.

This was an age of heroes. Just two months earlier, Charles Lindbergh, "Lucky Lindy" they called him, had flown the Atlantic non-stop. Even rural mountain people were in tune with the world by radio, and the people of Appalachia and the South were about to make hero celebrities out of three simple mountain people, the Carter Family.

With a hearty country breakfast under their belts, the four loaded up into Ezra's old Hupmobile and headed for Bristol. Rains had swollen the Holsten River at a place where they were to ford it, and the Hupmobile stopped right in the middle of the river and refused to go any further. Long dresses were hiked up over the ladies' knees, and guitars and autoharps carried on their shoulders to the dry bank, as the men pushed, struggled, and tugged until they finally got the old car moving. Up on the bank they discovered another problem; there was a flat on the right rear tire. A.P., being the flat-fixer, got out the hand

10. A.P., Janette, Announcer Brother Bill Rinehart, Sara, Maybelle, Helen, Anita, and June Carter. (Texas Radio Days, 1938-1939)
11. First Recording in August, 1927, in Bristol, Tennessee.
12. Maybelle played the Autoharp in a way that it hadn't been played before.
13. Ralph S. Peer

13.

6

14.

17.

15.

18.

16.

14. Helen Carter is the big sister of the Carter Sisters.
15. June Carter is the Comedienne of the Carter Sisters.
16. Anita Carter is the baby of the Carter Sisters.
17. When the Original Carter Family broke up,
    Maybelle formed a new group.
18. Mother Maybelle
19. The Carter Sisters practicing years ago.

19.

20.

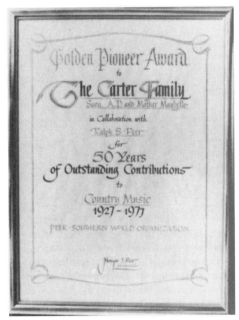

21.

22.

patch kit and quickly repaired the flat, pumped the tire up, and, with the instruments and the ladies aboard again, they made their way to Bristol.

Ralph Peer was immediately impressed with Sara's voice. As he put it, "As soon as I heard her voice, I began to build around it, and all those first recordings were on that basis." Peer had indeed found something special in Sara Carter. She had fine control, ingenuity, and she was a natural artist. With her background she could sing mountain blues, old parlor songs, ballads and love songs, and newer gospel and religious material. Paired with Sara's fine lead was A.P. singing the bass line and the accomplished Maybelle on the tenor

harmony, but Maybelle was mainly filling up all of the holes and laying down a bottom with her unique guitar style. Among the songs recorded that first day, August 1, 1927 in Bristol, were *BURY ME UNDER THE WEEPING WILLOW, STORMS ARE ON THE OCEAN, SINGLE GIRL, MARRIED GIRL,* and *THE WANDERING BOY.* Ralph Peer stated that all of the artists were paid $50.00 per song.

The Carter Family had always been in demand for personal appearances, but now, with the release of a phonograph record that was being played on the radio, their fame spread like wildfire and they were in demand all over Virginia, Kentucky, North Carolina, and South Carolina. More recordings followed. The recordings sold very well, so in May, 1928, the Carter Family was asked to come to Camden, New Jersey, the recording center for the Victor Company at the time. They recorded eleven songs and again in February of the following year, 1929, they returned to Camden for another recording session and recorded twelve more songs. Those sessions in Camden in 1928 and '29 were probably their strongest sessions, because in those sessions they recorded songs such as *DIAMONDS IN THE ROUGH, WILDWOOD FLOWER,* and *THE FOGGY MOUNTAIN TOP.*

As the children of the Carters were born and reached childhood, they were added to the live performances. Never fewer than three of the Carters performed, but sometimes the number reached as many as eight, including the very talented but little-recorded Janette,

A.P. and Sara's daughter. A Carter Family concert was usually a model of informality, the two women sitting in chairs with their instruments and A.P. standing. He would introduce the numbers after they had sung their opening number, which was a simple little homemade song that went:

Howdy do, everybody, howdy do
Howdy do, everybody, how are you
We are here we must confess
Just to bring you happiness
We hope to please you more or less
Howdy do.

A.P. was a man of few words. He introduced the songs and offered comments upon them, but very few at that. After the performances, the Carters would sell their song folios and would usually spend the night with newly-made

20. Jimmie Rodgers, Maybelle, A.P., and Sara Carter in Louisville, Kentucky, 1931.
21. Golden Pioneer Award presented to Sara and Maybelle.
22. A.P. Carter in Maces Springs, Virginia. A.P. died in 1960.

23.

friends who had come to their concerts. Hardly a concert passes that the Carters didn't make new friends, friends that they kept for their lives and in whose homes they would stay whenever they returned to that area. Doors in many homes were unlocked to the Carters.

Throughout the Depression, the Carters continued to record prolifically, certainly a test of their selling power, since most of the artists of the '20's were swept away with the lack of a record-buying public.

A.P. and Sara were separated in 1933, yet continued to work together with Maybelle. In 1938 the Carters went to Del Rio, Texas to begin a series of broadcasts that lasted for three seasons over XERA, XEG, and XENT, Mexican border stations that broadcast 500,000 watts. A.P. and Sara were finally divorced in 1939.

In 1939, Helen and June joined Maybelle, A.P., Sara, Anita, and Janette, who all performed on these broadcasts

23. Hall of Fame Induction - Maybelle, peermusic's Roy Horton, and Sara in 1970.
24. The Carter Sisters practicing.

24.

from time to time. At the beginning of their careers, the individual Carters led fairly routine private lives while each went his own way. Both of the Carter women had become mothers, each with three children, but the group got together to practice whenever they could, and were always together as a trio whenever the recording sessions came, although the sessions might be as far away as Camden, Charlotte, Louisville, Memphis, or Atlanta.

After leaving Del Rio, the Carter Family moved to Charlotte, where they spent a couple of years broadcasting over the station there and playing show dates at school houses all around. The Carter Family now was Mother Maybelle Carter, Helen, June, and Anita. From there they went to WRVA, Richmond, Virginia (1943-47), Knoxville (1948), and from there to Springfield, Missouri (1949). Finally, along with the guitar player they picked up named Chet Atkins, they moved to Nashville and the Grand Ole Opry in 1950. This became the Carter Family home—at least for the

25. Mother Maybelle and her mother.
26. Mom and Pop Carter
27. Mother Maybelle Carter
28. Helen, June, Anita, Pop and Mother Maybelle Carter

25.

26.

27.

28.

29.

30.

31.

32.

29. Early photo of Mother Maybelle and
    the Carter Sisters
30. Mother Maybelle, taken in 1973
31. Maybelle Carter, Sara Carter
32. Maybelle and Sara - August 1975 Reunion
    at Maces Springs, Virginia
33. The Carter Sisters and Mother Maybelle along
    with RCA Recording Artist Chester Atkins.

33.

34. Maybelle Carter was the backbone of the Carter Sisters and Maybelle group.

second generation of the family—for seventeen years as regular members at the Grand Ole Opry.

Sara moved to California with her second husband, Coy Bays. A.P. moved back to Virginia where he died in 1960.

Carter Family songs have become legends themselves, songs like *JIMMY BROWN THE NEWSBOY,* and *THE HOMESTEAD ON THE FARM.* They have become bluegrass staples, and continue to be sung at bluegrass and old-time gatherings all around the country. Joan Baez in the 1960's recorded Carter Family songs, beginning a new revival and a new interest among the young people in songs like *WILDWOOD FLOWER, GOSPEL SHIP,* and *LITTLE DARLING, PAL OF MINE.*

And wherever the old Carter Family songs are sung, the singer will often try to give a little history and background on the songs, in the tradition of A.P. Carter.

With the election of the Carter Family to the Country Music Hall of Fame, Maybelle, the last active member of the trio, enjoyed a period of acclaim worthy of her stature as a legendary founding member of our great country music empire.

Like A.P., Maybelle loved her native Virginia. Life in the arid Texas-Mexican border area was not her cup of tea. She longed to see the flowers on the green hillsides, to hear the rushing water of the clear mountain streams up on Clinch Mountain. She missed the smell of

hickory smoke curing the meat in November and she missed the snow in January. Her song, *LONESOME HOMESICK BLUES,* comes straight from the heart, for she wrote this song during their last season on the Mexican radio stations, shortly before she would return home to Clinch Mountain.

All these songs took the Carter Family off the slopes of Clinch Mountain and into the hearts of the world. During the time of Depression, they gave the country something to sing about. Turn up the sound a little and their presence will fill your room.

JOHNNY CASH

DIAMONDS IN THE ROUGH

Words and Music by
A.P. CARTER

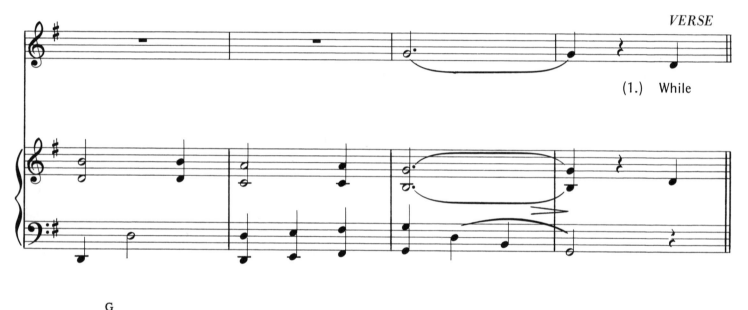

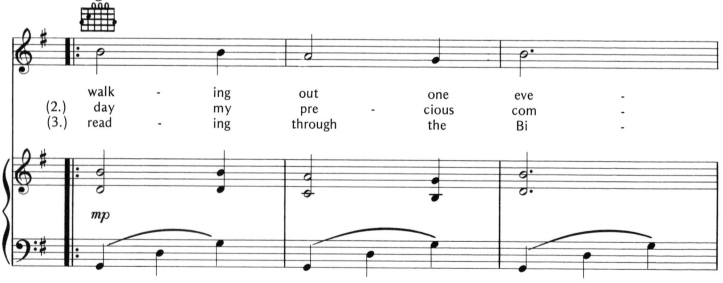

claim us all and says it is e-

nough_____ The dia - monds will be

shin - ing, but no long - er in the

1.2. rough._____ (2.) One

(3.) While rough. _____

3.

ENGINE ONE-FORTY-THREE

Words and Music by
A.P. CARTER

Moderately

G

(1.) A - long came the F. F. V., the
(2.) Geor - gie's moth - er came to him, a
(3.) Up the road she dart - ed, a -

C   G

swift - est on the line,_____
buck - et on her arm,_____
gainst the rock she crushed,_____

C
G
G7
quar - ters on the line, Re -
ing to make lost time, And
flames were roll - ing high; I'm
C
Cm
G
ceiv - ing their strict or - ders from a
if you'll run your en - gine right you'll
glad I was born an en - gi - neer to die
D7
1.2. G
sta - tion just be - hind.
get there just on time."
on the C. 'n O
C
D7
3. G
Cm
G
road.
ritard.
f

THE HOMESTEAD ON THE FARM

Words and Music by
A.P. CARTER

hear the cat - tle low - ing in the lane, You could

see the blue grass where I used to roam, You could al - most hear them cry as they

kissed their boy good - bye. I won - der how the old folks are at home:

(2.) Just a home.

35. The Original Carter Family

36. Maybelle, A.P. and Sara in Virginia

JIMMIE BROWN THE NEWSBOY

Words and Music by
A.P. CARTER

VERSE

(1.) You will hear me yell- ing, "Morn- ing Star,"__ as I
(2.) Nev- er mind, sir, how I look,_____ Don't
(3.) moth- er a- ways tells me, sir, _____ I've

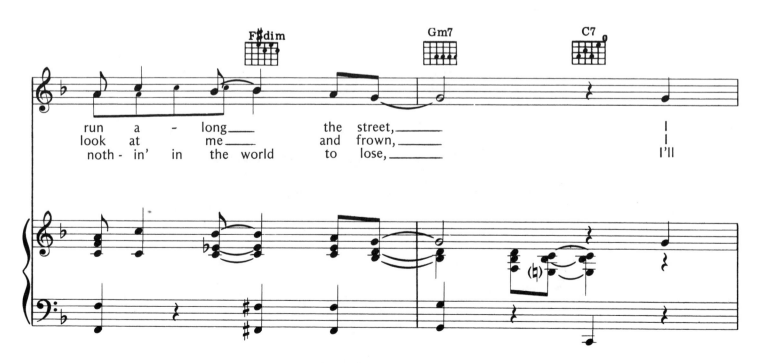

run a- long____ the street,_____   I
look at me____ and frown,_____   I'll
noth- in' in the world to lose,_____   I'll

CHORUS

place to place,__ my dai - ly bread to win._____ I
moth - er, sir,__ as I jour - ney on my way._____
pa - pers, sir,__ my name is Jim - mie Brown.____

sell the morn - ing pa - pers, sir,__ my name is Jim - mie

Brown, most ev - 'ry - bod - y knows I am __ the

news - boy of the town; (2.) town.
(3.) My

JOHN HARDY WAS A DESPERATE LITTLE MAN

Words and Music by
A.P. CARTER

KEEP ON THE SUNNY SIDE

Words and Music by
A.P. CARTER

LITTLE MOSES

Words and Music by
A.P. CARTER

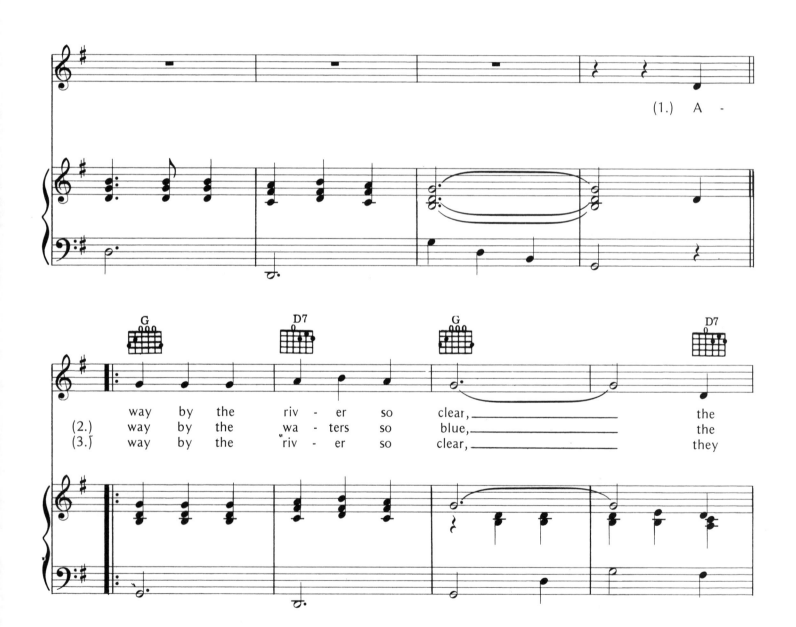

(1.) A -

way by the riv - er so clear,_____ the
(2.) way by the wa - ters so blue,_____ the
(3.) way by the "riv - er so clear,_____ they

LONESOME HOMESICK BLUES

Words and Music by
MAYBELLE CARTER

SINGLE GIRL, MARRIED GIRL

Words and Music by
A.P. CARTER

WABASH CANNONBALL

Words and Music by
A.P. CARTER

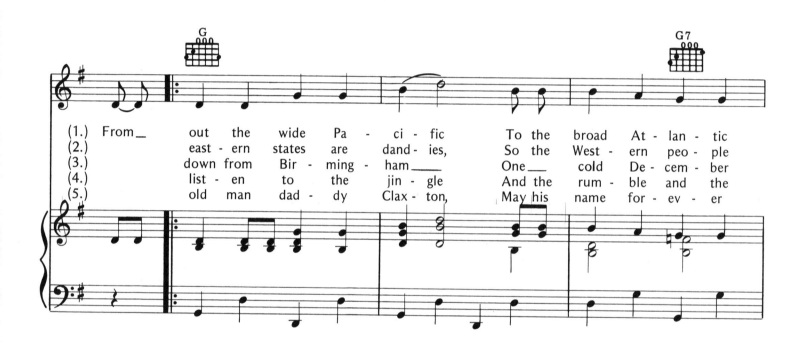

(1.) From__ out the wide Pa - ci - fic   To the broad At - lan - tic
(2.)   east - ern states are dand - ies,   So the West - ern peo - ple
(3.)   down from Bir - ming - ham__   One__ cold De - cem - ber
(4.)   list - en to the jin - gle   And the rum - ble and the
(5.)   old man dad - dy Clax - ton,   May his name for - ev - er

shore__ She__ climbs____ high____ mount-ains   Up____ hill and__ by the
say. When__ she climbed__ Old Rock   Is - land   Took__ all her__ style a
day. As she pulled in__ to the   sta - tion   You could hear all the peo - ple
roar, As she glides a - long the   wood-land   To the hills and__ by the
stand; May it al - ways be re - mem-bered   Through - out_____ the

WILDWOOD FLOWER

Words and Music by
A.P. CARTER

(1.) Oh, I'll

(2.)	twine	with my	min - gles and	wav - ing black	hair,	With the
(3.)	taught	me to	love him and	prom - ised to	love.	And to
(4.)	taught	me to	love him and	called	me his	flow'r.	That was

37. The Carter Family in the early thirties.